CW00820157

20319

GROSS JOBS
Working with
WATER AND SEWERS

by Nikki Bruno

raintree 🐾

a Capstone company — publishers for children

Raintree is an imprint of Capstone Global Library Limited, a company incorporated in England and Wales having its registered office at 264 Banbury Road, Oxford, OX2 7DY – Registered company number: 6695582

www.raintree.co.uk
myorders@raintree.co.uk

Edited by Hank Musolf
Designed by Bobbie Nuytten
Original illustrations © Capstone Global Library Limited 2019
Picture research by Heather Mauldin
Production by Katy LaVigne
Originated by Capstone Global Library Ltd
Printed and bound in India

ISBN 978 1 4747 7506 9
22 21 20 19 18
10 9 8 7 6 5 4 3 2 1

British Library Cataloguing in Publication Data
A full catalogue record for this book is available from the British Library.

Acknowledgements
We would like to thank the following for permission to reproduce photographs: Alamy: Zoonar GmbH, 18-19; Getty Images: Rick Meyer/Los Angeles Times, 23, ADRIAN DENNIS/AFP, 7, Chris Henderson, 4-5, John B. Carnett/Popular Science, 26-27, Yvonne Hemsey, 22; iStockphoto: andy_Q, 24 (inset), tzahiV, 14-15; Shutterstock: Gena Melendrez, 8-9, KaliAntye, 20-21, Kletr, 24-25, Kostas Koutsaftikis, 11, Peter Gudella, 17, Roman Demkiv, 28-29, Sherman Cahal, 12-13, Vladimir Mulder, cover. Design Elements: Shutterstock: Alhovik, kasha_malasha, Katsiaryna Chumakova, Liliya_K, Yellow Stocking.

CONTENTS

WORKING WITH WATER AND SEWERS

Imagine working with filthy water. Some water and **sewer** workers clean toilets and pipes. Others work in slimy, stinky tunnels. They get dirty to keep the rest of the world clean.

sewer system, often an underground pipe, that carries away liquid and solid waste

SEWER INSPECTOR

Sewer inspectors fix cracks and clogs in tunnels of waste. They wade through rivers of poo, wee, rotten food and dirty water. Sewers are also a favourite place for rats and other pests.

DON'T FLUSH THE WIPES!

GROSS-O-METER

Never flush wet wipes down the toilet. Wipes do not break down easily. Instead they combine with cooking fat. They create huge blobs called fatbergs. Sewer workers clear the clogs from drains and pipes.

A sewer inspector holding a fatberg in a London sewer.

SEA LAMPREY REMOVER

Lampreys are slimy fish with round, toothy mouths. They suck the blood of other fish. These gross **parasites** kill thousands of fish. Lamprey removers help the **environment**. They trap and remove these disgusting blood suckers.

GROSS-O-METER

DID YOU KNOW?

One sea lamprey can kill about 18 kilograms (40 pounds) of fish in its lifetime.

parasite animal or plant that lives on or inside another animal or plant and causes harm

environment all of the trees, plants, water and soil

OIL SPILL WORKER

Oil spills are messy disasters. To clean up the mess, workers skim off oil from the water's surface. They gather oily sand, seaweed, rubbish and wood. They also remove dead animals.

GROSS-O-METER

DID YOU KNOW?

The waste made by an oil spill is about 10 times the amount of the actual oil.

Workers cleaning up oil on a beach in Athens, Greece.

BRINE TANK CLEANER

Some homes have water softeners. Each one has a brine tank. It removes **minerals** from water. Over time, a foamy, brown mess of **bacteria** and dirt builds up in it. Brine tank cleaners scrub out this mess.

GROSS-O-METER

DID YOU KNOW?

"Hard" water is high in minerals. Soaps do not work as well with hard water.

mineral substance found in nature that is not made by a plant or animal. It has a crystal structure.

bacteria very small living things that exist all around you and inside you; some bacteria cause disease

BRINE TANK
#3

PLUMBER

Plumbers work with toilets, sinks and waste disposals. They have close contact with poo, wee, hairballs, vomit and rotten food. Some plumbers even find dead animals in drains and pipes!

GROSS-O-METER

DID YOU KNOW?

Some people clog their toilets with weird objects. One plumber in the United States pulled a live cannon round from the American Civil War out of a drain!

PORTABLE TOILET CLEANER

Portable toilets are helpful at parks and outdoor events. But people who clean them have a dirty job. Workers suck all the poo and wee into a big tank. Then they wash everything with a hose.

GROSS-O-METER

DID YOU KNOW?

Toilet seats are actually some of the cleanest surfaces in a bathroom. The floor is much dirtier.

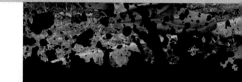

SLUDGE BUSTER

City buses get covered in oil, grease and dirt. When the buses are washed, this **sludge** falls into a pit. Sludge cleaners suck out the watery part of the sludge. They shovel the thick, stinky part into large drums.

GROSS-O-METER

DID YOU KNOW?

Bus drivers can avoid engine sludge by changing their oil regularly.

sludge muddy or slushy mixture

SEPTIC TANK REPAIR PERSON

Septic systems gather waste water from homes. They clean the water and release it into the soil. Water, wee, poo and rotten food collect in a tank. If the tanks clog or overflow, repair people come to the rescue!

GROSS-O-METER

DID YOU KNOW?

A septic tank must be pumped every three to five years.

CLOTH NAPPY WASHER

Workers drive around and pick up bags of dirty cloth nappies. At the factory, they dump the stinky nappies into big trollies. Then workers wash them. New workers often leave this job within hours!

GROSS-O-METER

DID YOU KNOW?

At a factory, one nappy might go through thirteen washing cycles to get clean.

WASTE WATER TREATMENT WORKER

 Some workers make dirty water clean. Raw sewage flows into water treatment plants. Workers use machines and chemicals to clean the waste water. Then they collect and test water samples.

GROSS-O-METER

DID YOU KNOW?

On warm days, people can smell waste water treatment plants from many kilometres away.

Waste water is cleaned in big vats.

HAZMAT DIVER

Imagine diving into filthy or oily water. This is the job of a hazmat diver. "Hazmat" is short for **hazardous** materials. Hazmat divers wear scuba suits. They clean waterways of raw sewage and dangerous chemicals.

GROSS-O-METER

SAFETY FIRST

Sewage can carry diseases. Hazmat divers get injections at a doctor's office. These **vaccines** stop them getting sick.

hazardous dangerous
vaccine medicine that prevents a disease

THANK YOU WATER AND SEWER WORKERS!

Water and sewage workers do things most people wouldn't. Thanks to them, waterways stay cleaner. They brave a lot of gross things to get their jobs done!

GLOSSARY

bacteria very small living things that exist all around you and inside you; some bacteria cause disease

environment all of the trees, plants, water and soil

hazardous dangerous

mineral substance found in nature that is not made by a plant or animal. It has a crystal structure.

parasite animal or plant that lives on or inside another animal or plant and causes harm

sewer system, often an underground pipe, that carries away liquid and solid waste

sludge muddy or slushy mixture

vaccine medicine that prevents a disease

FIND OUT MORE

BOOKS

How Things Work (See Inside), Conrad Mason (Usborne, 2009)

Loos, Poos and Number Twos: A disgusting journey through the bowels of history! (Awfully Ancient), Peter Hepplewhite (Wayland, 2016)

The Story Behind Toilets (True Stories), Elizabeth Raum (Raintree, 2010)

WEBSITES

www.bbc.com/bitesize/clips/z7jkjxs
Learn more about what happens to our sewage.

www.dkfindout.com/uk/science/amazing-inventions/ flushing-toilet
Find out more about the first flushing toilets.

INDEX